ARCHITECT

Miller Williams Poetry Series
EDITED BY PATRICIA SMITH

ARCHITECT

ALISON THUMEL

THE UNIVERSITY OF ARKANSAS PRESS
Fayetteville | 2024

ISBN: 978-1-68226-248-1
eISBN: 978-1-61075-817-8

28 27 26 25 24 5 4 3 2 1

Manufactured in the United States of America

Designed by Rachel Holscher

♾ The paper used in this publication meets the minimum requirements of
the American National Standard for Permanence of Paper for Printed Library
Materials Z39.48-1984.

Library of Congress Cataloging-in-Publication Data

Names: Thumel, Alison, 1991– author.
Title: Architect / Alison Thumel.
Description: Fayetteville : The University of Arkansas Press, 2024. | Series:
    Miller Williams poetry series | Summary: " 'When he died, my brother became
    the architect of the rest of my life,' writes Alison Thumel in Architect, which
    interweaves poems, lyric essays, and visual art to great emotional effect. In this
    debut collection, the buildings of Frank Lloyd Wright become a blueprint for
    elegy, as Thumel overlays the language of architecture with the language of grief
    to raze and reconstruct memories, metaphors, and myths. With obsessive and
    exacting focus, the poet leads us through room after room in a search to answer
    whether it is possible to rebuild in the wake of loss"— Provided by publisher.
Identifiers: LCCN 2023043782 (print) | LCCN 2023043783 (ebook) |
    ISBN 9781682262481 (paperback) | ISBN 9781610758178 (ebook)
Subjects: LCSH: Bereavement—Poetry. | Architecture—Poetry. | LCGFT: Poetry.
    | Essays. | Art.
Classification: LCC PS3620.H845 A893 2024 (print) | LCC PS3620.H845 (ebook) |
    DDC 811/.6—dc23/eng/20231108
LC record available at https://lccn.loc.gov/2023043782
LC ebook record available at https://lccn.loc.gov/2023043783

Supported by the Miller and Lucinda Williams Poetry Fund

The Props assist the House
Until the House is built
—*Emily Dickinson*

Contents

III. Perspective

Series Editor's Preface

The world has long flirted with implosion, and implosion has finally taken notice.

As I write this, we flail in a stubborn, insistent—and increasingly deadly—tangle of cultural, political, and global devastation. We once again speak of war as a given, a necessary and common occurrence. We're pummeled with unfiltered images of everything hatred can do, its snarl and grimace and spewed invectives, its stone in the pit of the belly. The air we breathe is no longer willing to nurture us, the earth no longer willing to be our unquestioning home. It's becoming increasingly difficult to find a direction that harbors solace or shelter.

And in the midst of our emotional desolation, we've been told—once again, dammit—that poetry is dead. It seems to die biannually, right on some crackpot schedule, its death often coinciding with the death of flared jeans, boy bands, and diet soda.

And once again—fresh from a deep dive into poetry that jolts, rearranges, rollicks, rebirths, convinces, destructs, and rebuilds—I am moved to dissent.

Poetry, at least the way it reaches me, has never been remotely close to quietus. It may occasionally be cloaked in a pensive or embarrassed silence or tangled in an overwrought and overwhelming barrage of language. It may be overly obsessed with sparing the delicate feelings of *someone* or maintaining the tenuous status of *something*. It can be tiring or inappropriate, or flat and studious, or heartless, or saddled with too *much* heart. Its pulse is sometimes so faint that its bare-there is often mistaken for that long-predicted demise.

At the biannual funeral, there is misguided celebration by tweed-swaddled critics, wheezing academics, and those who've spent their lives perplexed by poetry's omnipresent sway. It's a limit affair that makes them all feel better. But there's no weep or caterwaul, because actual poets—and gleeful lovers of sonnet, caesura, and stanza—have no reason whatsoever to grieve.

In fact, I come to you with reasons for rejoice, reasons to believe that poetry is not only alive, but that it is electric and naughtily raucous.

I must thank my tenacious and thoughtful readers, who consistently pass along the work that surprises, intrigues, and changes me. My readers are poets I revere—they are like me and unlike me, and the one thing they have in common is the consistency of their work. I've been contacted by people who say that the standard I've set for selection is virtually impossible.

I'm about to introduce you to four poets who seem, somehow, to have done the impossible.

Of course, picking a "winner" makes absolutely no sense in this context. Depending on the day and time I sat down to consider the finalists, their positions changed. The competition was just that heated. I want all of them to know, right now, that *any of you could have won.*

And all of them deserved to win.

Let's look at our—for lack of a better term—"runner-ups."

Adele Elise Williams's *Wager* was undoubtedly crafted to upend the familiar—both narratively and sonically—and turn it into something unflinchingly fresh. Language, as some of us know, exists to be fiddled with, and Williams, a storyteller who steadfastly refuses lyrical compliance, has a grand ol' time reintroducing us to what we assume we already know. I love a poet who runs rampant, rebelling against restraint—however, that by no means indicates a lack of discipline or a desire to cloak the work in "device." These poems hit home because they pull us into the poet's rampaging narrative, because we are all creatures of story who crave POVs that rouse us and redefine what we see. As a former "performance poet" (whatever that means these days), I took particular joy in reading *Wager* aloud—more than once, more than twice— and reveling in what Williams's deftly crafted ditties do to the air.

I mean, this is the opening of "Gal," the *first poem in the book*:

> She's so helpless and the undertone
> is spooky-ooky! She's so natural
> and the assumption is heaven high
> is gilded and gyrific, is like chakras.
> I mean, placement for purpose. I mean,
> outward burst. She's so blond!

And if that aural deliciousness puts you in the mood for play—not so fast. These poems swirl with shadow when you least expect it. The next time poetry dies, I highly suggest a massive infusion of—this.

Self-Mythology, by Chinese-Iranian poet Saba Keramati, is the book we need right now, as so many of us explore our hyphenated selves, searching for meaning in being not all one and not all the other, wondering if and where we are truly rooted.

But even as we turn inward for clues, we're a suspicious, judgmental lot, and so much of the volatile confusion that marks our days springs from a brash selfishness—our unwillingness to consider the person next to us, to learn what that person feels and believes, the tenets they live by. Keramati first confronts the formidable task of knowing the body and mind she inhabits—her backdrops and looming future, her vulnerabilities and failures, her reactions to loss and love, the experience of being two in the body of one. In her poem "The Act," she writes, "I'll always be / here, chameleoning myself // with every shift of the light."

So many writers are telling these stories—or making their best attempts to. Keramati avoids the many pitfalls of addressing a complex identity—you won't find confounding DIY tanglings of language or an unwavering eye fixed on the myriad metaphors of culture clash. *Self-Mythology*'s poems unreel with revelation, undaunted soul-searching, and crisp, deliberate lyric:

> Let me write myself here, with these symbols
> I claim to know, swear are in my lineage—
>
> proving myself to my own desire
> to be seen.

To be seen. To be heard. To grieve and rejoice and question out loud. All while so many demand a Black silence.

It has been decided, obviously by those who decide such things, that Black folks have made entirely too much noise about inconsequential things like—well, history. Our collective history, and the history of each one of us, the past that won't stop quivering in our chests. All those histories hastily being rescripted. Refocused. Disappeared.

In the midst of a country's fervent undertaking to render the Black voice inconsequential to both that country's backdrop and its future, Jeremy Michael Clark's insistence upon light—troubled though it may be—is imperative and rebelliously wrought. The huge story rests within the smaller one. Clark chronicles the fevered intersections of love and fear, and whole restless worlds reside in each line. Truths are unrelenting here—plain truths that agitate as they enlighten. There's so much of our lives that we hastily bury, hoping all that restless mayhem stays settled beneath us.

Clark, however, will not allow our conjured calm. Although there's a tender, assured turn to his lyric, he remains steadfastly focused on what trouble does to the light. His search for father is heartrending. Consider "Those That Flew":

> Before the house I believe is my father's
>   I stand, a rust-flecked fence
>
> between me & the answer. A latch
>   I can't lift. Rain comes & I say,
>
> *Is this how it's supposed to be?*
>   Soaked, unable to shield myself
>
> from what puddles at my feet.
>   I don't carry his name the way
>
> I have his silhouette. Thunder sends birds
>   scattering & I count the seconds
>
> between each clap to gauge how fast
>   the storm will come, though clearly,
>
> it's here. From my mother
>   I learned my name. I know
>
> their song, but not what I should call
>   those birds that flew.

You may think you've wandered this narrative landscape before. But you haven't. Not in this way.

And finally, the winner of this year's Miller Williams Poetry Prize—Alison Thumel's *Architect*.

I can't describe this book. I fill up every time I try. There's very little language huge enough to illustrate the depth of the poet's grief, her stark and tender transforming of it, her clenched containment of it as it pulses and bellows, straining to escape its borders.

There are so, so many ways to speak loss, but I've never experienced such structured tenderness, the building and rebuilding of what crafted the hollow. Alongside poems about Frank Lloyd Wright's creations, those glorious and lasting bodies, Thumel searches relentlessly for a lasting body her brother John might inhabit.

She has written often of John's death, and anyone who's barely lived through that grim upheaval will instantly recognize that anguished search for anything other than its bone-numbing torment.

Thumel builds and builds and loses and loses. And begins to build again.

> Here I mark the spot where desolation
> ended and began. Yet why mark this spot
> if marking only remakes a misshapen
> memory of the wound? The mark is dotted
> like a line to form a charred and ugly
> scar I run my fingers over, this path
> I trace. Ended and began. Ended—see
> I can mark the bounds of it. Nothing past
> this wall I build, each brick a stitch I slip,
> a slit I suture. Nothing—like trying
> to see into a dark room before I dip
> my hand far into that place. No small thing—
> no stone, no wood, no work made of absence—
> could mark you back into a present tense.

There are no words for what these words do.
And that's what it means to love poetry.

PATRICIA SMITH

ARCHITECT

Prairie Style

In fall, the milkweed
stood past our waists.

I was small, and you
were smaller, two pods

growing in a row:
pods we plucked

and pierced
with stems of berries,

giving little red eyes
to green parakeets.

Holding them, silent
between our palms,

we didn't notice
a hawk overhead.

Tearing them open,
we found feathers

waiting inside.
Inside a memory

is its ruin.
Inside ruin, what?

I

Plan

Every great architect is—necessarily—a great poet.

—*Frank Lloyd Wright*

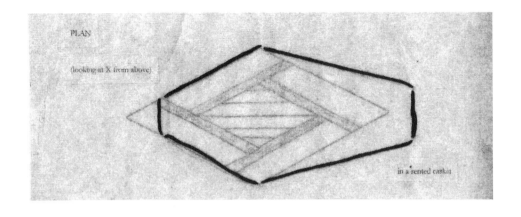

coping

(n.) The capping or covering of a wall that protects the parts vulnerable to water damage

So what if the building still stands.
I too have water problems,
So what if the building still stands.
grief directional as a swelling.
So what if the building still stands.
So what if the building still stands.
The swelling forms an outline,
So what if the building still stands.
stain of living.
So what if the building still stands.
So what if the building still stands.
If living is maintenance, I regret
So what if the building still stands.
the structure I'm maintaining.
So what if the building still stands.
So what if the building still stands.
Maintained echo. Inside me,
So what if the building still stands.
a load-bearing frame, shifted.[1]
So what if the building still stands.

---

1. [I]n our opinion there could be no feeling of complete safety and consequently we recommend that the proposed site not be used for any important structure. (*Fallingwater Engineering Report*, 1936)

Q:

How are you coping?

A:

Five years after my brother's death, I audited an architecture class on Frank Lloyd Wright. The professor allowed me to take the class on the condition that I do all of the required work. *But I'm a poet,* I wrote to the professor. *I've never built anything before.* I purchased graph paper. I took notes. I traced the lines along with the professor's steady hand in the soft, smeary pencils that Wright preferred. *Wright liked to play with confinement and release,* I heard on a tour of a Wright house many years later. Like birth, I thought. My brother was born in Oak Park, Illinois, not far from Wright's home and studio. Three weeks before he died, he and I watched bats taking off from beneath a bridge. (Confinement. Release.)

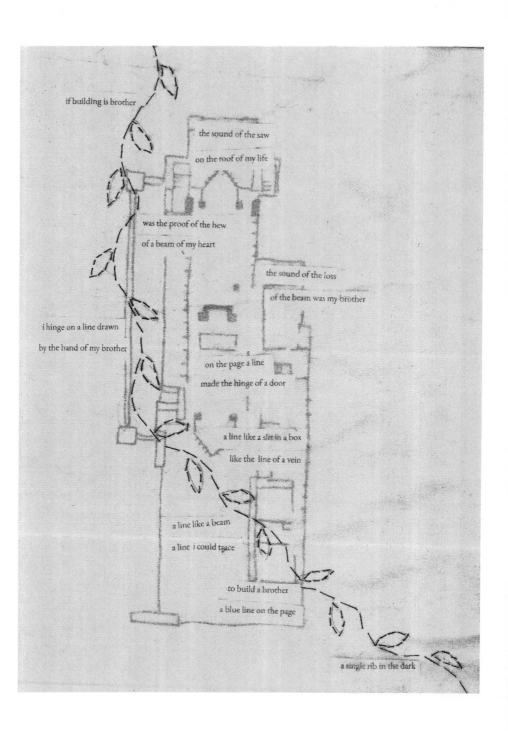

if building is brother

the sound of the saw

on the roof of my life

was the proof of the hew

of a beam of my heart

the sound of the loss

of the beam was my brother

i hinge on a line drawn

by the hand of my brother

on the page a line

made the hinge of a door

a line like a slit in a box

like the line of a vein

a line like a beam

a line i could trace

to build a brother

a blue line on the page

a single rib in the dark

A:

I came to the class believing that if I could not write about my brother, perhaps I could build something that could carry weight. I may have been searching for a new metaphor, to get away from night-dark fields and twisted metal. I remembered that stanza means *room* in Italian. Maybe I believed that if I could not cross the threshold of my grief, perhaps I could build one, wall it off in separate rooms, and choose whether or not to enter. How easy it is to say, *When he died, my brother became the architect of the rest of my life. Grief became the house in which I live.* Yet my brother was an engineer, not an architect. In the book about why buildings fall down, I read, *A much better metaphor for a building is the human body.* Metaphor should appeal to the senses, I tell my students, because it's hard to grasp what you cannot sense.

*Like most human bodies, most buildings
have full lives, and then they die.*

[Revision]

    Bodies have lives.
    Human buildings.
    Like bodies, full, and then.
    Most die.

Fig. 1

Robie House (1909–)
Chicago, IL

All our childhood was a prequel
to construction—sky bent
around mountains of dirt, the field

behind our home plowed under,
our voices drowned out by the rumble
of trucks—that unfinished backdrop
against which I can build any memory:

the roofs rising in right angles,
the streets sketched onto a grid.
Cul-de-sac, we learned. Subdivision,

like the math I fought against
at school each day. (What is subtracted
if I don't recall you? What division
existed even then?) The line drawn

between our yard and the field
gone to seed, the grass knee-deep.
We had never seen real mountains—

a mountain was anything
that blocked our view.

[See also: Prairie Style]

A:

An engineer and a poet lie beneath a bridge. The poet says, *Look how you can see the bats against the sky as an absence of stars.* And the engineer says, *Flight is only a matter of surface area.*

A **wing** is a part of a building subordinate to the main or central part of the structure.

In the Prairie Style, most floor plans took on a cruciform shape, with four wings extending out from the central hearth, creating a division between public and private spaces. (How could so many wings give the illusion of flight while staying so low to the ground?)

[See also: flyover state]

A:

In a poetry workshop, someone asked if the brother in my poem was a metaphor. I thought of the way I tell my students that metaphor is not just decoration for a poem, the way Frank Lloyd Wright once said, *A doctor can bury his mistakes, but an architect can only advise his clients to plant vines.* Perhaps the nature of metaphor is in abstraction, in the distance that it creates. The way Wright did not build a replica of a sheaf of wheat, a hollyhock bud, a honeycomb, but an abstraction of these. The way I can write the shape of the thing but not the thing itself.

GLOSSARY OF TERMS
Organic Architecture

black blood collects in his ear like a teeming hive
but dad notices his hair. he cut it just last week.
i study his neatened neckline and sideburns,
evidence of a recent close shave, as if preparing
for a school dance or a job interview, clipped
a bit too short at the top, all cowlick, expecting
in a week or two it would lie down just right.

A:

A certain Wright house I knew well fit snugly on a narrow Chicago lot, its roof slung as if shading its eyes, the long low eaves meant to mimic the prairie, though this was the city. A place always knows what it once was—like a person always knows where they are from. For years after my brother's death, I collected news articles on people who died young and tragically in landlocked states. Prairie Style deaths—boys sucked down into grain silos or swept up by tornadoes or fallen through a frozen pond. The boys I didn't know, but the landscape I did. The dread of it. How many miles you can look ahead. For how long you see what is coming.

Prairie Style

The way this beach is no good for surfing, riptides swirling the color of salted asphalt.

The way we question the sand and whether it was brought in from somewhere

because of the way the grains skid down the dune as kids turn somersaults from the peak.

The way they never seem to reach the ground, just like the planes passing over this state.

The way the boy was backlit in the noon sun and then gone, the sand giving beneath him.

The way he was sucked down like a finger in fresh cement.

The way they dug him out barely breathing, sand filling his lungs like ballast.

The way this could be called a landlocked kind of drowning.

The way scientists dug up the dune to find a web of roots rotted to nothing.

The way they hypothesized the forest that once towered there had been swallowed up.

The way sand rushed in to fill the space left by decay.

The way a breath can be mistaken for a similar lack.

The way the doctors picked the grit from the boy's throat grain by grain.

The way the boy lived though they called it impossible.

The way we talk about leaving

       even as the parts of us we uproot keep growing back underground.

A:

I found the Wright house gutted, the floors stripped
to the concrete's quick. The docent spoke of res-
toration when she meant replica. *Painstaking,* she
said of the attention to the moldings. Putting it
back to the way it was before was what she meant,
but everything was new. Philosophers talk about
the Ship of Theseus, its planks replaced one by
one. Architects call this preservation. Poets call
this revision.

GLOSSARY OF TERMS

Preservation —

maintaining as it is

(if my brother were here)

Restoration —

reverting back to its original state

(if we went back in time to my brother)

Rehabilitation —

fixing any flaws or structural damage

(if we could have fixed my brother)

Reconstruction —

recreating what was destroyed by disaster

(if we could bring my brother back)

[Revision] —

If I could build a brother,

I would build him differently.

Over Speakerphone

FAST Fiberglass Mold Graveyard – Sparta, WI

Driving hours north, a forest with a black river. A river steeped
dark as tea. Tannins bleeding off the roots. Roots thirsting

over distance. A distance that dulls my voice. Over speakerphone,
my mother isn't listening. The not-listening moves at seventy miles

per hour, traveling away. Away from her, she reminds me,
counting the years. I count the little casualties littered along

the county road like mile markers. A dozen porcupine, more
possums. I call my mother weekly. Weak broth, brackish baths.

She's dieting, feels better. Field mouse, flattened frog, smudge
I cannot name. Names the new DiCaprio film, total crap.

Cracked vase at the cemetery. Reminds me I've never been.
Beans struggling in the garden, though the peppers are prolific.

She's proud. Too many, pickled to last the year. Torn ribs
of tires, raccoon cubs blunted in a row. Rolling static. I miss

something about the neighbors, something about the Pope.
Doe's skyward hooves like an upturned table. New kitchen set,

dark wood, heart-soft tomatoes, endives. Diving swallows
framed in dust, half-moon of the windshield. Wind farm,

mown field, all our men. Hem of clouds dropping. Dropped
call's quiet. I stop in a clearing sown with hollow forms.

How can I know a thing by the shape of its absence? At my feet,
a dragon's open mouth. Dropseed in the furrow of its tongue.

II

Elevation

Where scenes of horror had identified the structure
with ugly memories, I changed it all.
—*Frank Lloyd Wright*

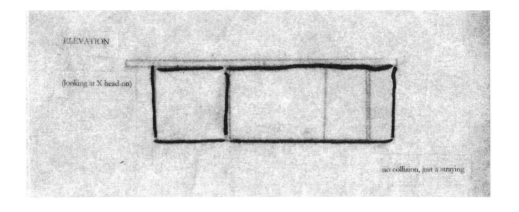

ELEVATION

(looking at X head-on)

no collision, just a straying

sistering

(n.) To affix a new beam to a damaged one as a supplemental support

if a beam is not solid · fit it with a sister
lay her body down · alongside the one
with a fire-scarred face · damp-wracked cheek
black knot of an eye · blinking flat back
what is the purpose · in this fixture
we call mourning · the motion spent
in maintaining · what we can't afford
to cut away and risk · the roof and what
makes maintenance · more rational than
the inevitable ending · hammers falling
with no breath · no peace at night
my spine held fast · in quiet inversion
to a buckled shape · slung behind me
call me sound · and sister-joined
and i'll say this · from the rafters
i hear my mother · asking me again
if i wish for burial · or burning
a granite niche · in a wall next to him
the correct answer · always the one
i do not give—no · i did not choose
this way i rot beside · him anyway—look
still i am holding up · this falling house

Q:

What does sistering mean to you?

A:

I knew the ship before I knew the myth. I knew the ending before I knew the characters. But isn't the myth always the same? The hero slays the monster—

◆

—and we forget all the details. Once, on an island, there was a monster that the king trapped in a labyrinth. Or, once, a king was forced to make a choice between killing his wife's monster-child and offering up the children of others as sacrifice. Or, once, the monster's sister helped the hero slay the monster. All of these parts exist simultaneously and yet are interchangeable.

◆

But as I said, I knew the ship before I knew the myth. The ship the hero sailed on was docked in the harbor as they paraded him through the streets. Over time the hull rotted, each plank removed and replaced with a board with a new arrangement of knots like eyes in its surface.

A:

All myths have a body count. Wright's love Mamah was murdered in the home he built for her— Taliesin, the house perched on the brow of the hill. In the history of the house, the mythology of its tragedy seems to matter more than its walls. My mind skips over the bloody prose of it—the house aflame, the residents fleeing, each felled with a hatchet at the threshold. *Felled like a beam,* I thought, for this was easier than thinking of bodies.

Taliesin I (1911–1914)
Spring Green, WI

Here I mark the spot where desolation
ended and began. Yet why mark this spot
if marking only remakes a misshapen
memory of the wound? The mark is dotted
like a line to form a charred and ugly
scar I run my fingers over, this path
I trace. Ended and began. Ended—see
I can mark the bounds of it. Nothing past
this wall I build, each brick a stitch I slip,
a slit I suture. Nothing—like trying
to see into a dark room before I dip
my hand far into that place. No small thing—
no stone, no wood, no work made of absence—
could mark you back into a present tense.

A:

Taliesin destroyed by fire, read the telegram to
Wright. No mention of the fate of his love, as if it
was more useful to focus on the thing that could
be salvaged. What beams could be pulled from the
smoldering pile.

◆

(Why am I stuck on this? The color of her dress,
the wording of the telegram, the way it must have
looked like lightning struck, though the papers say
it was a clear day. I think that it is easier to face the
stories I've heard before than the ones I'll never
know.)

Whirling Arrow

The house was on a hill. I could see all directions
        in a single moment. The ground fell away beneath me.
That was the illusion, of stepping into nothing.
        Two pieces of glass met in an invisible way, an arrow
in the air. I thought I could put my hand through.
        My hand knocked like a bird into the pane. One

day passed into another. Down a long passage, one
        room into another. This house the largest gift directed
my way. I must have been contained by it. Through
        shelter I was sheltered. This man's house for me
to replace another man's house. My life an arrow
        drawn back and released by a man. I said nothing

to this. Some only saw my figure in relation. Nothing
        allowed of me but a squared frame over which one
softer figure could bend. But. Does not an arrow
        make an arc out of a line. Does not direction
telling us we do not bend make fools of us.
        I bent to love. I was a fool. I was pierced through.

I remember it. The house on a hill I ran through.
        The door open to the golden fields. If nothing
bent, you could see forever. That was the end of me
        falling over the horizon. The sun in the sky at one.
Toward love, I bent. All my life in one direction.
        A threshold crossed with difficulty. Like the arrow

drawn though my skull. No matter it was not an arrow
        but another edge. Toward love, and through,
I thought. Everything must be cut in the direction
        of the grain. The sun, the grain, the field, then nothing.
At the threshold, I was cut like a beam. I became one.
        I became something you could build on. Making me

was a more violent motion of remembering. You and me.

      Two beams meeting in a visible way. Each corner an arrow
pointing outward. As I've said, to cut a thing is one
      way to build. You kept building until you saw it through.
To build another woman for this shelter. Nothing
      like what became my tomb. She comes and goes in all directions,

through a threshold of my bones. The house, without me
      will not stand. My aim is jealous as an arrow bent to nothing.
When one beam burns, you see smoke from all directions.

A:

Someone once told me that in order to be a myth,
a story must have a degree of *inevitability*. In death
there is always innocence. Not a thing could have
gone differently. Here is how Wright mourned:
he began rebuilding Taliesin the next day.

◆

(I have lost my way in this metaphor, all of these
stories overlapping. They run together. I am no
longer sure whether I am Ariadne, or if I am the
architect. I cannot determine whether my brother
is Theseus or the monster, whether he is the
mistress or the house. The inevitability of either
conclusion.)

Taliesin II (1914–1925)
Spring Green, WI

No poem or words can rebuild an absent
body. They only mark its bounds. No past
I write is truthful as the present tense.
Lies I run my fingers over—a page
I wrote in the dark. I mean, *lines.* The neat
lines I form of the charred and smoking
truth. I mean, each line is a death I cheat.
I stitch up the end to the beginning,
splice both with my sutures. I try
to end where it began. To close the gap
grief made. To count the years in lines.
To make my memory into a map
without a key (must I have one?)—listen:
X marks the spot of my devastation.

A:

I am trying to trace my way back to my brother in my memory. This story unspools before my eyes, the memory never neatly wound. The winding of this thread spelled so like *wound,* something to stitch up.

◆

A king and an architect are trapped in a labyrinth. The king says, *Are you sure this maze can hold any being?* And the architect says, *If my plan accounted for a way out, I wouldn't still be in here.*

◆

Perhaps this labyrinth is one I have built myself, like this metaphor, a ship I have folded out of paper and just as watertight. It feels like, in myth as in the stories we tell of my brother, we are missing pieces. All of our lives warped completely. A single missing plank is enough to sink a ship.

In the past, blueprints were created using a
_____ process. Photosensitive ink was
spread on a sheet of paper over which the
original drawing of the floorplan was placed.
When exposed to light over an extended period
of time, the background on the created paper
would turn blue while the spaces blocked from
light by the drawn lines would remain white. In
this way, the blueprint shows a presence with
absence—the lines of the blueprint not shown
with darker ink but with a blank portion of the
page. In this way, _____ hollow being left, the
outline of which the sun is not able to reach.
Underground, another place where the sun
does not hit. Today, other faster processes are
preferred for blueprint creation.

Taliesin III (1925–)

Spring Green, WI

Oh, my desolation is misshapen—
I admit, in present tense, I anger
in almost infinite combinations.
Those slit sails or round bricks I rearrange
into easy shapes that match what they think
my grief should be: a quiet mourning dove.
Here is what I know it as: a blinking
bird of prey, a darkening star above.
If I begin and end in present tense—
cast my map past any mark of you—
still your end loops over any sense
of my beginning. What does anger do
but search for marks of curse or godsend,
when maybe there is nothing to amend?

[See also: Ship of Theseus Paradox]

A:

When I visited Taliesin, I expected to see a trace like a scar on its surface. I found no signs of death, though they were pointed out to me. The seam where a blown oak had fallen through the ceiling. Heat-blistered beams visible at an angle through a ceiling grate. Remains of an old wall. Rooms built on the footprints of past rooms, hovering over each other like ghostly blueprints. I saw no trace of blood, none of the violence, the myth and poetry of it.

◆

Another solution to the paradox: I am rebuilding a life that will never be the same.

◆

When Taliesin burned down a second time, years later, Wright again rebuilt it. The tour guide noted that each time Wright rebuilt the house, he never created a replica of what had been lost in the fire. Instead, he gradually added to or subtracted from or changed the plans. In fact, Wright made no blueprints for the house. Preservationists are measuring it inch by inch, mapping the house in its entirety, its precise shape. Recreating a floor plan that was never there to begin with.

Sistering

How many angles   from which I could see this coming.
All the men in this family die young   my brother says.

Gliding over the cobblestones.   I try not to step on the cracks
as if articulating the rule   creates the gap for exception.

Not me. Not this—   on the phone on my knees
sun dragging into the sky.   Not this—

a brother swerving   the chariot too hard
golden wheels lapping dirt   into embers. Not this—

golden reins severed   soot bowing the sky
darkening arc of a body.   Every myth has brothers

pierced by arrows.   Every myth has sisters
lined up like neat pearls.   Sisters crying so long

they turn into poplars   leaking bright beads of amber.
Sisters, a flock of guinea fowl.   A constellation of stars.

If this were myth   I would already be transformed.
I do not know what I am   or what I might become.

III

Perspective

[Y]ou are not really reliable. You will say a thing is so when you only think it is so. You will promise and not keep it.

—*Frank Lloyd Wright, letter to his son Lloyd*

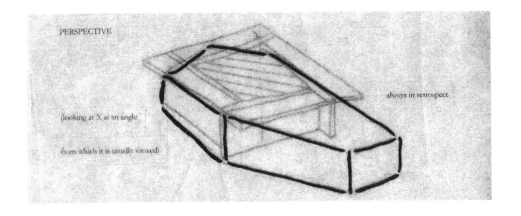

heroic

(adj.) An attempt at rebranding brutalist architecture, covering up violent meanings with ones intending to underscore the style's architectural and structural merits

Two grasshoppers fuck in the fresh black mulch.
I don't know that. I'm five and I don't know
what fucking is but I know grasshoppers
and their notability. I run to tell my grandmother
about the grasshoppers stacked like Jenga blocks.
I'm full of precarious joy and summer watermelon.
She carries my brother so he can see them, too.
He sees them fucking. He's unimpressed.
He looks at my expectant face. His foot lowers
and then slides as if wiping gum from his shoe.
My grandmother meets my sobbing screams
with revisions. His disinterest was disappointment.
His cruelty was irrelevant. The grasshoppers
were gone before he ever moved to hurt them.

Q:

Why are you writing him as a hero?

A:

In the days after the accident, reporters contacted my parents and my brother's friends for comment. Not a single one contacted me. The relief I felt at this, but also the anger. As if I could not memorialize him properly.

◆

I've seen Fallingwater's engineering report, the calculations of whether the value of something is worth the maintenance it requires, or the risk.

◆

The turn of the poem is always where we are headed, the swerve I write over and over again.

Fig. 3

Usonian Home (1937)

(shown here with migraine and flashback, other repeatable structures[2])

The blue vein in my head beats a well-worn track.
        Remembering is like a pinhole at the end of a tunnel.

One prick and the pain opens wide as a funnel.
        Salt, white light. Doctor tells me *Track your triggers.*

July, blonde boys. Therapist tells me to track what triggers
        the pictures I never saw. The car, flipped.

Next moment, a reel running, a flipped switch.
        I swallow a pill to numb the nerves, pull curtains shut.

What I swallow climbs my nerves. But with eyes shut,
        blurry wreckage. My tender thought. Some other

blood I've wreaked. A leak in my brain. Another
        day spent with forehead pressed. If I could I would

apply pressure before the thought. I would tell
        the blue vein to beat forward instead of back.

---

2. Course Notes

An attempt at a simple, repeatable house for middle-class Americans, the Usonian home was never truly repeatable, as Wright wouldn't give up personalization, leading to designs that were always custom and over budget.

A:

Wright's buildings were beautiful but unreliable, though their unreliability was forgivable. To praise Wright's work is to praise an idea and how it came to life, but not its living. The way people praise a poem they do not have to live inside.

◆

Years before the accident, my father said he would trust my brother with his life. He thought trust was the same as reliability. But one must be proven, and one must be broken. The way at the wake I knelt on the July-hot asphalt to light matches one by one in the funeral home parking lot. Reliable: the way the match always bent into the flame.

◆

Perhaps I am an unreliable narrator. Perhaps I've been so concerned with the ship I've forgotten the whole myth, the many branches of it growing out and out like vines in a labyrinth.

A:

In every myth, in every memorial, I now search for
the body count of it, the stories we have heard but
have never traced back to their hero.

Aegeus, who leapt from a rocky
cliff to his death.

Ariadne, whom Theseus left in
the night.

Icarus, who burned.

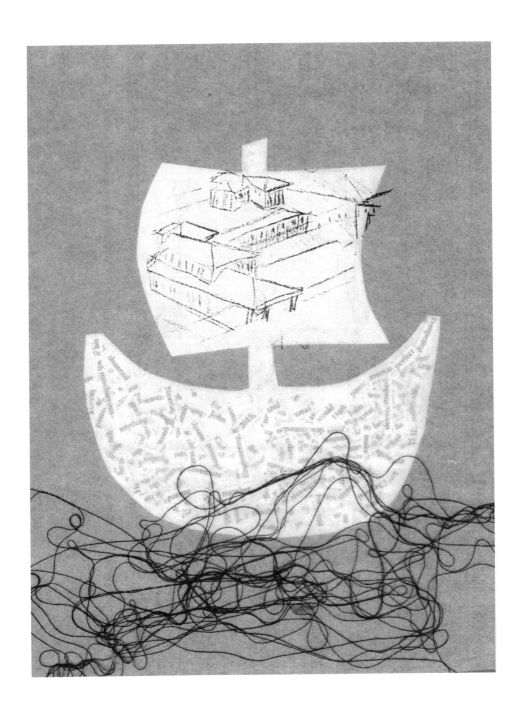

A:

I don't want to write this as an elegy because it comes out too beautiful, with none of the sharp rocks at the edges. So much damage around the hero like a cracked foundation. We notice the ship in the harbor, but not the body floating offshore, the flaming comet falling from the sky, the glint of a mirror signaling from a far-off island.

My father at the edge of the cliff
of his grief.

My mother watching the wings
she built burn.

My future, with water on all sides.

lintel

(n.) A horizontal support spanning an opening in a wall, such as a door or window, which is a vulnerable point in a building's structure

When my mother falls through the ceiling,   I believe it
without seeing   the fistfought mouth of the drywall.

She was alone. I believe it.   I can picture my mother
marching backward   into lack. My mother, caught.

My mother, from above   consumed. From below,
a breech birth. My mother   with a ceiling fanned

around her waist   a ballerina-skirted fracture.
My mother's legs   a chandelier that darkened,

lattice of broken veins   lathed beneath her skin.
My mother saying nothing   until weeks later,

saying the ceiling is mended, her hip   still tender.
She says the drywall   got the worst of it. How much

we do not talk about   when we are pretending
to believe everything broken   can be fixed quick.

A:

Here is another myth: Wright designed Fallingwater in two hours after his client surprised him with a visit to check on the designs. If this is true, then perhaps our origin stories mirror our declines. What blind trust we place in our heroes as the floor falls down beneath us. The inevitability we admit in the maintenance: without these stories we tell ourselves, we could never survive.

◆

If Fallingwater's sagging metal skeleton was not replaced, it would have tumbled down the waterfall. I can't help but see the inevitability. *Form forever follows function,* Wright's mentor taught him.

Fig. 4

Fallingwater (1935–)
Mill Run, PA

Falling back into this water. Felt the swelling, thick wet lumber. Tongue gone heavy with explaining. Peering closer, risk the spill back down the squall. Like a pier off Fallingwater. Built it off the waterfall. Wouldn't stand or couldn't bother. Last saw my brother down by the water. Bats alighting. Watched the swelling. Bridge stretched out over the water. Sky black with wings like darkened water. Then saw him pumped full of salted water. Could not believe it, death denier. Numb as plaster. Feeling nothing like disaster. He held the water. Kept the pressure. Steady rush up to the heart. But— Couldn't keep it. Falling pressure. Oh Fallingwater. Body balanced off the hearth. Cantilever, death defier. Balconies all set to clatter, all my platters held aloft. Too delicate, this arm of life. Living room or waiting room, then down the water. Falling rush of hollow pressure. Felled by water. Can't remember. Cutting flow I follow back. I fall again. The cataract. Swollen slash of swollen river. Crash returned to. Well I worry. Deep within me, self-filling. Welling falter, self-fulfilling. No wall to fix. No failed form. Could not keep the water out.

[See also: Ship of Theseus Paradox]

A:

It is easier for me to anger than to mourn, but it is far easier to write an elegy than a condemnation. If a house is meant to offer shelter, why build one that could crumble? If a hero is meant to save us, why do so many minor characters not survive the story? I have heard that surviving siblings are often called forgotten mourners. I too am a minor character. If I make you a hero, what will that make of me?

◆

If I could I would take the side of those who said that Fallingwater should have never stood. And yet I wonder what it would be like to believe so strongly in something. To believe with such certainty that the flag was the right color, that the balcony wouldn't give way under my weight. To memorialize someone unequivocally, without footnotes.

Memorial Day

The chain lift scrapes the undercarriage, spitting a click-clack-click as it drags the car
to the top of the roller coaster's first hill—setting us up for a ninety-degree drop
that will sustain a speed of seventy-five miles per hour for three minutes.
This part of the ride makes more noise than seems necessary, metal
on metal making a protest or a prayer: *Do you hear me, horizon?*
I'm coming for you, too. Across town, my grandfather cups
a hand to his eyes to survey the new hydroponic farm.
They're tearing up good farmland there, he points
to the greenhouses dark with vines, gleaming
in the late afternoon sun, a mile beyond
fields of corn not yet ankle-high.
The glass houses surrounded
by stones dug up by backhoes seem
to him the start of a parable. Every house
in the neighborhood waves a flag from the eaves
and the old man next door killed his wife, my grandma
tells me, but not on purpose, blacking out, his car kissing
the guardrail too hard, and hadn't he never let her drive anyways?
The lift hill's teeth-rattling din is meant to feel like nostalgia. Though
they laid new track, they left the old wooden bones underneath. At the base
I'd felt like a big fish bucking against its reeling in. Now, near the top, I lean back
and let my eyes turn to the dark-blue sky. My mouth widens to a scream. We plummet.

A:

An architect, an engineer, and a poet stand at the top of the waterfall. The architect says, *You will hear the rush of water from every room.* And the engineer says, *I think that's a liability.* And the poet says, *It will be beautiful when it falls.*

◆

Even I pray for stories of redemption. In the hospital, I begged again and again for the doctors to donate his heart, as if this would be the proper ending to the story, a hero's ending: a single plank of the original body built up into a ship that would one day float.

◆

Here is what I know: when tourists visit Fallingwater, they can't see the waterfall from inside the house. Here is what I mean: I never could have saved you. Here is what I write: I'd like to think the last thing you remember is the night sky, white stars arranged against a blue page. As if ending on an image leaves this parting open.

Sistering

last week the cottonwoods shed fuzzy tufts

overnight the ground was carpeted

in weightless piles children scattered

with galoshes on the way to the bus

the week before it was the apple blossoms

there then gone again in three short days

seeing another season without you

sliding by me like a screen door

this season i learned the word ambiparous

i mistook the word to mean having both

leaves and flowers growing simultaneously

one after another from the same stem

though it better describes possibility

a bud's capacity to produce two structures

blossoms the opening act for leaflets

a beginning that echoes a small death

in humans parous defines a number

of offspring a woman produces in a lifetime

our mother would be ambiparous

if this word were used for more than flora

if you had not been taken in a false spring

if you the bud's first bloom came in

hot and brief like blood to a fresh wound

if i am the slow green encore

Notes and Acknowledgments

"Floor Plan" poems
In section I, the book referenced throughout the "Floor Plan" series is *Why Buildings Fall Down* by Matthys Levy and Mario Salvadori (Norton, 2002). The quoted text is from the book's introduction.

The Wright quote in [Floor Plan: *In a poetry workshop*] was often used by Wright in various lectures and interviews during his life, often with slight variations in phrasing.

In section II, quoted lines are from Frank Lloyd Wright's autobiography.

"Taliesin I"
In 1914, an employee at Taliesin murdered Wright's mistress Mamah Cheney, her children, and several other employees of Wright's; the murderer then set Taliesin on fire. In his grief over Mamah's death, Wright rebuilt the home he had originally built for her; over the next several decades he continued to rebuild, modify, and add to the home.

This poem is a partial cento, with several lines and phrases from the chapter of Frank Lloyd Wright's autobiography describing the Taliesin tragedy. The other Taliesin poems further deconstruct and rework these lines.

"Whirling Arrow" and [blueprint with labyrinth]
The title of the poem and the embroidery of the blueprint reference the "Whirling Arrow" pattern designed by Frank Lloyd Wright.

"Usonian Home"
This poem uses an interpretation of Jericho Brown's "duplex" form; however, most Usonian homes were simplex.

"heroic" and [blueprint with ship]
These poems use text from my brother's obituary, which I wrote in 2015.

◆

Architectural definitions throughout are adapted from Wikipedia, *Merriam-Webster,* and the Designing Buildings Wiki.

Quotes from Frank Lloyd Wright are from:

- *The Future of Architecture* by Frank Lloyd Wright (Horizon Press, 1953), 8.
- *Frank Lloyd Wright: An Autobiography* (Duell, Sloan and Pearce, 1943), 26.
- Frank Lloyd Wright, in a letter to his son Lloyd, excerpted in *Many Masks: A Life of Frank Lloyd Wright* by Brendan Gill (Da Capo Press, 1998), 43.

These poems reference an architecture class at the University of Wisconsin–Milwaukee taught by Professor Mark Keane in fall 2020. The visual poems in this book use architectural drawings I created during the class.

Some of the poems, at times in earlier forms or under different titles, have appeared in *Indiana Review, Ninth Letter, Poetry,* and *Sugar House Review.*

I am grateful to the Elizabeth George Foundation, whose grant allowed me to travel to several Wright homes, as well as to the MFA program at the University of Wisconsin–Madison and the Stegner Fellowship at Stanford University for providing time, space, and financial support during the writing of this book.

This book would not exist without the support, feedback, and encouragement of so many people over the years. To my professors, workshop-mates, friends, and family: thank you for believing in this book, and thank you for believing in me.